Keeping Unusual Pets

LIZARDS

Peter Heathcote

Heinemann
LIBRARY

www.heinemann.co.uk/library

To order:
☎ Phone 44 (0) 1865 888066
🖹 Send a fax to 44 (0) 1865 314091
💻 Visit the Heinemann bookshop at www.heinemann.co.uk/library to browse our catalogue and order online.

First published in Great Britain by Heinemann Library, Halley Court, Jordan Hill, Oxford OX2 8EJ, part of Harcourt Education.
Heinemann is a registered trademark of Harcourt Education Ltd.

© Harcourt Education Ltd 2004
First published in paperback in 2005
The moral right of the proprietor has been asserted.

Editorial: Nancy Dickmann, Louise Galpine and Tanvi Rai
Design: Ron Kamen and Celia Floyd
Picture Research: Rebecca Sodergren
Production: Séverine Ribierre

Originated by Dot Gradations
Printed and bound in China by WKT Company Limited

ISBN 0 431 12416 7 (hardback)
08 07 06 05 04
10 9 8 7 6 5 4 3 2 1

ISBN 0 431 12421 3 (paperback)
09 08 07 06 05
10 9 8 7 6 5 4 3 2 1

British Library Cataloguing in Publication Data

Heathcote, Peter
 Lizards. – (Keeping unusual pets)
 1. Lizards as pets – Juvenile literature
 I. Title
 639.3'95

A full catalogue record for this book is available from the British Library.

Acknowledgements

The publishers would like to thank the following for permission to reproduce photographs:

Bruce Coleman/Animal Ark: p. 6 (top); Bruce Coleman/Kim Taylor: p. 22; FLPA/Silvestris Fotoservice: p. 11; Maria Joannou: p. 45 (bottom); NHPA: p. 9 (bottom); NHPA/Daniel Heuclin: pp. 5 (bottom), 40 (bottom); NHPA/J&A Scott: p. 4; NHPA/Karl Switak: p. 35 (bottom); OSF/Brian Kenney: p. 11 (bottom); OSF/David Fox: p. 5 (top); RSPCA/Stephen J Divers: pp. 37 (top), 37 (bottom), 39; RSPCA/Ken King: p. 19; SPL/CNRI: p. 36; SPL/David Scharf: p. 40 (top); SPL/Sinclair Stammers: p. 38 (bottom); Tudor Photography: pp. 6 (bottom), 7, 8, 9 (top), 10, 12, 13 (top), 13 (bottom), 14, 15, 16, 17 (top), 17 (bottom), 18 (top), 18 (bottom), 20, 21 (top), 21 (bottom), 23 (top), 23 (bottom), 24, 25, 26, 27, 28 (top), 28 (bottom), 29 (top), 29 (bottom), 30, 31 (top), 31 (bottom), 32, 33 (top), 33 (bottom), 34, 35 (top), 38 (top), 41, 42 (left), 42 (right), 43, 44, 45 (top).

Cover photograph reproduced with permission of Tudor Photography.

The publishers would like to thank Yarnton Nurseries for their assistance in the preparation of this book.

Every effort has been made to contact copyright holders of any material reproduced in this book. Any omissions will be rectified in subsequent printings if notice is given to the publishers.

Contents

Any words appearing in the text in bold, **like this**, are explained in the Glossary.

What is a lizard?

Lizards are one of the oldest groups of animals alive today. They lived alongside the dinosaurs 230 million years ago during the **Cretaceous period**. Lizards are part of the animal group called **reptiles**, which is made up of several thousand different **species**.

Several characteristics make reptiles different from other animals. First, reptiles are cold-blooded or **ectothermic**. They cannot internally control their own body temperature. If the air gets too cold, then lizards slow down and eventually go into a deep sleep. Second, reptile skin is not elastic like human skin, but tougher and rougher, with no hair. This makes it more difficult for a lizard to control its body temperature. Lizards do not sweat, like humans, so they cool down in other ways. A lizard's body temperature will change depending on its surroundings. To cool down they move into shaded areas of their environment, and to warm up they **bask** in the sunlight.

Komodo dragons are the world's largest lizards. They can be up to 3 metres long and weigh 70 kilograms!

Lizards' eyes, as well as their skin, are also different to those of **mammals**. They have no eyelashes to filter out dust in the air, but, unlike snakes, lizards can close their eyes. Lizards also have an external ear opening as well as an eardrum. They cannot hear sound as well as humans, but they can detect pressure-waves. If you call to your lizard it will hear what you say, but will probably not come running to you!

4

Your responsibilities as a pet owner:

- Never buy a pet without first considering the good as well as the bad points.
- Young children are not allowed to buy pets. Take an adult along with you to the pet store.
- Never buy a pet because you feel sorry for it.
- Check that your pet is **captive-bred**. Taking animals from the wild means that fewer lizards are able to rear young and keep their species alive. By purchasing captive-bred animals you will not impact upon the wild population. Captive-bred animals are more likely to survive and flourish in captive conditions and should not have the **parasites** that are often found in **wild-caught** reptiles.
- Insure your lizard. Your local **herpetological** society will offer advice. Health insurance for animals means that if your pet becomes unwell you need only worry about looking after it, and not about the cost of treatment.

A lizard's eye has scales all around it but no eyelashes.

Lizards love to bask in the sunshine. Sunlight helps them to produce vitamin D3 in their skin to keep them healthy.

Lizard facts

There are thousands of types of lizards living all around the world. They have adapted to life in very different locations, with a huge range of diets and **habitats**. However, many lizards do not make suitable pets and it may be necessary to have a special licence before they can be taken home. One such lizard is the **komodo dragon** which has poisonous saliva in its mouth and can grow to a massive 3 metres long!

Bearded dragons

Bearded dragons are one **species** of lizard that do make good pets, provided that they are well cared for. This book is based on bearded dragons but the care advice applies to most other kinds of pet lizards too. The **genus** to which bearded dragons belong is called *Pogona* and comprises many species, each with subtle differences. Two types of *Pogona* are *Pogona vitticeps*, the inland bearded dragon, and *Pogona barbata*, the coastal bearded dragon.

Pogona vitticeps (top) and *Pogona barbata* (bottom) originate in Australia and can be found across a wide expanse of territory.

6

Lizards as pets

Before purchasing a bearded dragon you need to consider its typical, daily behaviour. Bearded dragons may be kept in a small group, but unless you intend to **breed** them, it would be better to keep just one. If you plan to keep more than one, remember that males will fight if kept together.

On introducing a cage-mate both lizards may start to wave their arms, as though greeting each other. This arm-waving, however, is simply a means of communicating with one another and assists in establishing **territorial** claims as well as dominance or submission.

A bearded dragon waving its arm to communicate.

Your pet may occasionally puff out and darken its throat (or beard). This happens in both male and female animals and shows that they are distressed or annoyed. Normally, when the beard darkens, the bearded dragon will bob its head up and down to make itself look more impressive.

Pogona vitticeps grow to a length of 20 centimetres, snout to vent (this means without the tail!), whereas *Pogona barbata* grow to 25 centimetres, snout to vent. Both species can live for over seven years in captivity, so taking on a bearded dragon really is a long-term commitment.

Important advice

- Never put two male bearded dragons together.
- Never put two animals of different sizes together.
- Always have a veterinarian check a new pet before introducing it to another one.

Is a lizard for you?

Before you purchase a bearded dragon you must think very carefully. Is a bearded dragon the right pet for you? Are you the right person to own a bearded dragon? It can be very disappointing when you realize that the pet you wanted is not a realistic possibility, but it is better to understand this before you buy the pet and make it unhappy too.

Bearded dragon good points:

- They can live for over seven years.
- They can be handled every few days.
- They can be purchased as babies and you can watch them grow.
- They only need feeding once a day.
- They only need to be cleaned once a week (spot cleaning should be done daily).
- They don't make any noise to disturb the neighbours.
- They become tame very easily.

Although they aren't soft and furry, lizards can be handled on a regular basis.

Bearded dragon not-so-good points:

- Bearded dragons carry diseases that can be passed on to humans (**zoonoses**) unless routine hygiene precautions are taken.
- They require artificial heat to **maintain** their body temperature; this means that long walks outside are difficult, except on the very warmest of days.
- It can be very expensive to set up a bearded dragon's **vivarium**.
- It is sometimes difficult to obtain the varied diet required to maintain a healthy bearded dragon. This will need time and effort from you.
- Veterinary treatment is expensive and finding a veterinarian experienced in treating **reptiles** can prove difficult. If your pet is sick, you may have to travel in order to find someone who can help.
- You will need to keep insects in your home and there is a chance that some may escape!

Lizards like to eat lots of creepy-crawly live food. Are you willing to keep crickets in your house?

Some kinds of lizards, like this Thorny Devil Lizard, are clearly very unsuitable to keep as pets!

9

Choosing a bearded dragon

It is very difficult to select a bearded dragon from a brief meeting at the pet store. You will have many questions that need answers. Most importantly, before you commit to purchasing your new companion, stand back and take a good look around the store. What do you see?

DO NOT TAP ON THE GLASS

Things you should see:

- Well-**ventilated** cages
- 'Guarded' heat sources protecting the animals inside from burning themselves
- Thermostats controlling the heaters; this makes sure that the occupants don't get too hot or too cold!
- Insects on sale should be in good condition. Poor food will mean poor pets!
- Clean cages with fresh water
- Specimens should be **captive-bred** with feeding records available
- **Ultraviolet** lights should be fitted.

Have a good look at the lizards and the cage they are in at the pet shop before you buy one.

Problems to watch out for:

- Mites or ticks on cage occupants
- Dirty water bowls
- Dirty cages
- Lack of thermostats or ultraviolet lights
- **Wild-caught** specimens.

One or two dragons?

It is perfectly acceptable to keep one bearded dragon on its own. It will not feel 'lonely' or 'sad' as long as you make sure that it is in the correct environment.

Male or female?

If you do not plan to **breed** your pet, then it is best to keep a single male dragon. Females can have health problems if they are not allowed to breed, and may need expensive veterinary care should they be unable to pass their eggs. Remember, many female lizards will lay eggs even if they do not have a mate.

Buying your bearded dragon

The best place to buy your dragon is from a private breeder. If you have problems finding someone in your neighbourhood, why not join your local **herpetological** society who should be able to help you? You should always take an adult with you when buying a pet.

Top tip

Bearded dragons like cool fresh water to drip onto their heads, allowing it to run into the corners of their mouths for drinking.

Male and female lizards look very similar so make sure you check what sex your pet is before you buy it.

Juvenile bearded dragons are very delicate and should be handled with great care.

11

What do I need?

A **vivarium** is a cage in which reptile-keepers house their pets. You can buy them at pet shops or make your own. In a vivarium you can control the warmth and **humidity**, and make sure that live food cannot escape into your home. It is also important not to let a lizard run around your home unsupervised. Remember that **reptiles** can carry diseases that humans can catch. Also, your lizard may be accidentally injured by curious family pets.

Materials

Use wood as the main construction material in the vivarium, except for the front of the cage where sliding glass doors (toughened and rounded at the edges to prevent nose-rub) will allow you easy access to the interior of the cage. A wooden construction will help the cage maintain the correct temperature. A dark wood will also help to reduce the effects of **stress**. All internal joints should be sealed with silicon rubber to help prevent both the leakage of water and an **infestation** of mites, which can **breed** rapidly in any small gaps.

A wood vivarium with sliding glass doors is an ideal home for a lizard. What other things are needed to make the cage comfortable?

All the wooden edges of your vivarium should be sealed with silicon.

Shape and size

Ground-dwelling animals, like the bearded dragon, prefer a vivarium that allows them room to investigate and move around, behaving as they would in the wild. A vivarium measuring 120 centimetres long, 60 centimetres deep and 45 centimetres high should be adequate for a single lizard.

Ventilation

The amount of **ventilation** in the vivarium will depend on humidity requirements. Ventilation can be achieved by drilling holes in the back or side of the vivarium. These should be placed at the top and bottom of the enclosure in order to provide an airflow. Air holes should be less than 5 millimetres in diameter, so that lizards and their insect prey are unable to escape. Vents should not be placed at the same height opposite each other as this creates a draught in the cage, which may lead to sickness.

Air vents like these allow fresh air to enter the vivarium.

13

Heating

As an **ectothermic** reptile, your pet must have its body heat controlled artificially. You should create a warm area and a cool area in the cage. The warmest area which your lizard will use for **basking**, should be between 31 and 35°C. Place the heaters towards one side of the vivarium, rather than in the middle. Heating supplies are easily available from pet stores and online supply companies. There are three main types:

- Ceramic heaters – these get very hot and must be shielded
- Spot bulbs – use only dark colours as bright white will distress the animal
- Heat mats – should cover less than one third of the cage-base; your lizard must be able to escape the heat if it wants to.

Safe basking areas are essential for your lizard's well-being. Notice that the heat source is shielded using a metal frame.

You will need:

- A thermostat to control the heat
- A securely fastened guard over all heat sources to prevent your pet from burns
- To ensure that the animal is not small enough to pass through the gaps in any wire mesh guard
- Thermometers to keep a check on possible thermostat faults.

Humidity

Humidity is the amount of water in the air. Low humidity can cause problems for reptiles when shedding their skin, and also with their breathing. Humidity meters are available from hardware stores and should be used to maintain levels around 35 per cent. Remember that ventilation will alter the level of humidity; an increase in ventilation will decrease humidity and vice versa.

What happens if the humidity is wrong?

- Respiratory problems (breathing difficulties)
- Skin problems: blisters and infection
- Eye infections
- **Infestation** problems: mites, ticks and flies.

Check the humidity meter and thermometer regularly to ensure ideal conditions inside the vivarium.

Lighting

There are three main types of lighting used for reptiles:

- **Ultraviolet** (UV) encourages healthy bones and muscle control.
- Reflector bulbs (combined system) can be used with other heaters in larger cages.
- **Incandescent** bulbs can be used to create localized heat spots and are available in a variety of wattages. For a 120 centimetre long vivarium, a 100 watt bulb will be required (remember this must be attached to a thermostat). The bulb should be placed at one end of the vivarium in order to make the largest temperature change from one end of the enclosure to the other.

Ultraviolet

UV helps many animals to produce vitamin D3 in their skin, which is then converted internally to the active vitamin D3. Without D3 reptiles are unable to absorb calcium. UV lights should be left on for ten to fourteen hours daily and replaced every six to nine months. There are several models of UV tube available which have fewer harmful side-effects than the older type of tube. Check with your local **herpetological** society.

Reflector bulbs

If used as a heat source, dark-coloured bulbs can be used at night to provide a night-time effect. Dark-coloured bulbs can be used during the day in conjunction with an UV source to give a daylight effect.

Bulbs will require changing periodically so keep a spare one to hand.

If bulbs are used to create a 'hot spot' then turn them off at night, as long as another heat source **maintains** the background temperature. A wire guard should cover all reflector bulbs. A pattern of day and night time effects can reduce stress-related problems. Remember that your dragon will become distressed if it lives under white light for 24 hours a day, seven days a week. It is important to recreate the most natural conditions possible. In the wild your lizard **species** will have been used to a regular pattern of day and night.

You will need to move your lizard to a clean, temporary home before you start cleaning out the vivarium.

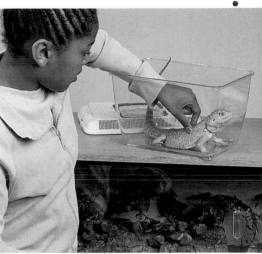

Hygiene

To prevent problems with **parasites**, make sure that all joins in the vivarium are filled with a silicon sealer. This stops mites and eggs getting stuck inside the vivarium joins. The vivarium should be regularly cleaned with a mild disinfectant. Pay particular attention to corners, and dry it well before replacing your reptile. After handling animals and cleaning out the vivarium, make sure that you wash your hands with a mild disinfectant or antibacterial soap. Food and water bowls should be removed, cleaned and replaced daily. Do not place food and water containers from the cage on surfaces in your kitchen as this may spread disease.

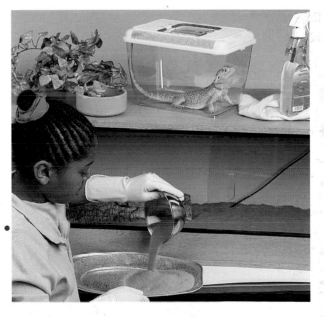

Use a mild disinfectant to clean out the vivarium. You must wear rubber gloves when cleaning.

Substrate

Substrate is placed at the bottom of the vivarium to absorb lizards' waste products. Some substrates are brightly coloured to decorate the cage; others, such as orchid bark, maintain high humidity. You should remove any soiled substrate from the vivarium and renew it completely on a regular basis.

Bearded dragons love digging, so good quality substrate is essential to keep them happy and healthy.

Lizards live well on calci-sand, sold in pet stores. Be careful not to use sand containing silica, as it will **dehydrate** your reptile and can kill it. Bags of children's play-sand are often sold as 'silica-free' and are less expensive than specially produced sands, but remember to check the label! Any substrate can cause problems if swallowed by your pet.

Plants

Real plants look attractive in the cage, but check that they are not poisonous to reptiles. Plastic plants often break into smaller pieces and can be easily swallowed, causing a blockage in the bowel. Information about safe plant species is constantly updated and you should check this with your local herpetological society.

Green plants in the vivarium make it look nice and give your lizard lots of places to hide.

Cage furniture and hides

Furniture provides **hides** to help the lizard feel secure within the cage, and reduce stress-related problems. Remember that it is your responsibility to help your new pet live a happy, relaxed life, so make sure it has plenty of hiding places.

Hides can be made from a variety of items such as cardboard boxes with holes cut in the side, plant pots, purpose-made caves and anything hollow, even the inner section of a toilet roll! A heavy rock, that is completely stable and cannot be moved by your pet, can also be placed in the vivarium. Make sure there aren't any sharp edges as they can injure your animal.

Hides are important in encouraging **hatchling** lizards to feed – if your reptile feels unsafe it will stop feeding. They should be placed in each of the warm, medium and cool areas of your enclosure. Do not place the hide only in the coolest part of your cage as a dragon will always choose security in the hide over warmth. It is best to place one hide in the middle of the cage neither too close, nor too far, from the heat source.

In the wild, lizards often hide between rocks and cracks to feel secure from predators and to escape the heat from direct sunlight.

Caring for your lizard

There are several different foods that are suitable to feed to your bearded dragon. It is important to change your pet's food at different stages in its life. **Hatchling** dragons will eat a different diet to that of adults.

Remember to feed the insects fresh fruit and vegetables before you feed them to your lizard. Make sure you keep the box closed tightly!

Your dragon is an omnivore.
This means that it will eat both meat and vegetation. Examples of live food include fruit flies, mealworms, crickets, waxworms, small locusts and garden insects. Small mice can be offered as an occasional treat (these are available ready-frozen from pet stores).

What to feed?

Before we consider what to feed your new pet, also think about preventing diet-related illnesses. Make sure that the insects you feed to your dragon have been 'gut loaded.' Place the insects in a secure container with fruit and vegetation for at least 24 hours before being fed to your pet.

Top tip

Never defrost reptile food in hot water; place it in a sealed container in a cool area to thaw out slowly. A refrigerator is the best place to defrost your lizard's food items.

Salad should make up 20 percent of your dragon's diet.

Hatchlings

If you have purchased a hatchling dragon (aged from birth to three months) then offer him small crickets (around 9 millimetres long) three times a day. Offer as many crickets as your lizard will eat before losing interest. These should be live to attract its attention. Do not leave any uneaten insects in the cage. This is tempting on a busy day, but can result in an annoyed pet, as uneaten insects jump around your lizard.

The salad you offer should be as varied as possible but avoid dark greens such as spinach, as they upset the calcium levels in the body. Broad leaf watercress and dandelion leaves are both suitable.

Food can be used to tame your lizard. Always use tweezers when feeding your pet by hand in order to avoid accidental bites.

Top tip

Avoid feeding mealworms to hatchling bearded dragons as they are very hard to digest and may cause death.

Juveniles

Once your lizard is four months old, feed it less often. Try offering medium-sized insects twice daily. If your pet shows little interest in the second feed, then offer food only once. Make sure that salad is offered every 48 hours and never leave pieces of salad in the enclosure for more than 12 hours. As your pet grows, the amount of salad it needs will increase to around 50 per cent of its food.

Mealworms can be offered to your pet once it is over four months old. Use a variety of insects even if your lizard prefers one sort to another. Be careful with the size of food you offer your pet; as a general guide the food must always be smaller than the widest part of your lizard's head.

Adults

Once your lizard is 18 months old, it is considered an adult. Adult dragons eat a wider variety of foods, including small mice, king mealworms and adult locusts.

Top tip
Always place salad in the coolest part of the cage.

Adult dragons' feeding can be reduced to every couple of days. Keep a close check on your pet and if it starts to look thin, increase its feed. Record what food it is eating: remember that its survival depends on you.

Always remove the back legs of locusts before you feed them to your lizard. They have a sharp piece that can stick in the lizard's throat.

Vitamin and mineral supplements

In captivity lizards may not receive all the necessary elements of their diet. The most important mineral for bearded dragons is calcium carbonate, due to its role in supporting muscle **contractions**. This should be mixed into the salad as well as coated on any insects offered to your pet. If you fit a good quality **ultraviolet** tube to your cage, then no supplements will be needed apart from the pure calcium carbonate. Do not put any commercial vitamin or mineral in drinking water as it changes the taste and discourages your pet from drinking.

Top tips

- Place a small amount of calcium powder in a plastic bag, put insects inside and shake the bag gently until a coat of calcium covers the food.
- Remove the water bowl and offer the insects to your dragon. Once it has finished replace the water bowl and return any uneaten insects to their cage.

A plastic bag can be used to mix up food and supplements.

Remember to place fresh water in the vivarium every day.

23

Treats

A tasty treat for a bearded dragon is the waxworm, though these should be used only as a treat, and not as a dietary staple. Never offer cat food or dog food to a dragon as this causes liver and kidney damage and can kill your pet. An occasional spoonful of pet food will have no long-lasting effects, but it is best to avoid it.

Skin and nail care

When your lizard starts to shed its skin, spray a gentle mist of warm water over it to help the process along. Once it has shed, make sure that no pieces of skin are left on its toes or around its tail, as these could restrict its blood flow.

The nails on your pet will need to be cut regularly so that they don't scratch you when you are handling it. You can use a pair of ordinary nail clippers but be careful not to hurt your lizard or make its toes bleed. Ask a friend to hold it still and only remove the very tip of the nail, usually less than 1 millimetre. This will need doing quite frequently. You can help your lizard file its own nails by putting rocks with different surfaces inside the cage for it to crawl onto and scratch.

Make sure that you never cut more than a millimetre off when trimming the lizard's nails.

Holiday care

It is never a good idea to leave your pet alone while you go away on holiday, even if it is just for the weekend. Always ask a responsible person to take care of your dragon. Pet stores and **herpetological** societies can suggest someone experienced in caring for bearded dragons.

Checking your bearded dragon

It is very important that you check your pet regularly to make sure it is well.

Check that:

- your lizard has no mites or ticks on its body or in its cage
- there are no unusual lumps or swellings particularly around its mouth
- no skin is stuck around its toes or tail
- its eyes are clear and bright and its nose is not blocked.

The box that your pet travels in should only be slightly larger than the lizard itself.

Taking your lizard to the veterinary surgeon

If your lizard gets ill you will need to take it to the veterinarian. Place your lizard in a container only slightly larger than itself. The box should be strong, well-**ventilated** and clearly marked with the words 'This way up'. Keep the box out of direct sunshine and draughts, and never leave it unattended. Lizards can die in hot motor vehicles, so plan your journey well and keep your pet with you at all times.

HANDLE WITH CARE!

Can we make friends?

Reptiles are wild animals that have only been bred in captivity for a fairly short period of time. They are not as friendly as dogs and cats. However, most **captive-bred** bearded dragons are **hand-tame** from a very early age and respond well to gentle handling for short periods of time. It will take time for your lizard to know your scent; remember lizards do not respond to recognition in the same way as many other domestic pets.

Be gentle and take your time!

When you first select a dragon, remember to choose from a few that are healthy. Once home, make sure that you wait before you start to handle and get to know your new friend. For the first week you will only be able to watch your lizard and feed it. It is tempting to pick it up and show it to your family and friends, but this will not allow it enough time to get used to its new cage.

Let your lizard get used to you slowly. Just watching it instead of picking it up will also help you to understand your new friend's habits much better!

After the first week of patiently feeding and caring for your new dragon comes the time to handle it for a few minutes. Gently lift it out of the cage in a warm room and sit on the floor with it on your hand. Make sure you are in a room where it can easily be caught if it runs away! Time how long you have it out of the cage; remember that it depends on its cage to keep its body warm. After ten minutes put it back gently and offer it some food. Never handle it immediately after feeding or you may make it **regurgitate** its food.

How to pick up your lizard

Pick up your lizard by placing one hand under its stomach and then, supporting its full weight in the palm of your hand, scoop it up. Remember not to make any sharp jerky movements, as this will make it think that you could be a **predator**. Never pick a lizard up by its tail, as this can cause it damage!

Always support your lizard's body when you handle it.

Meeting other lizards

It is not a good idea to introduce your bearded dragon to other lizards. Unlike **mammals**, bearded dragons do not feel the need for sharing or company; they will not feel sad if they are housed alone for their entire lives. But if you still want to introduce your lizard to others, make sure that they are female and of a similar size. Also remember that healthy-looking animals can still carry diseases that are not yet making the animal sick.

Never let your pet meet other animals such as dogs and cats. They may not intend to hurt it but may think it is a toy and injure it while playing. Whatever type of **vivarium** you are using it is important to make sure that all access panels, whether they are from the top or the front, are securely locked.

Be very careful when you introduce your lizard to another lizard – they are not used to having much company.

Always keep the vivarium shut securely, especially if you have other animals in the house.

28

Harnesses and collars

Many types of harness are available from pet stores. If you find a suitable lizard harness it will allow you to take your pet outside during warm, sunny days. Natural sunlight is better than all of the artificial **ultraviolet** tubes in pet stores and this will be very healthy for your pet.

Top tip

Natural sunlight may change your lizard's personality. It may change in a flash from being friendly to aggressive!

Biting

It is very rare for captive-bred bearded dragons to bite their owners. If this happens it is probably an accident at feeding time. Remember not to feed your pet with your fingers. Place food items close to it but leave enough time for you to remove your hand. If you are bitten, dragons will often let go straight away. If they don't, then try not to pull your hand away, as this will cause more damage to the skin.
Be patient and it will let go after a short while. Make sure that you use a mild disinfectant on the bitten area once the lizard has been removed.

Keep your distance when you feed your lizard.

29

Fun time together

Bearded dragons do not play in the same way as domestic pets; they won't fetch your slippers and they are very slow to learn new tricks! Some animal behaviourists believe that you can train lizards, but in reality it is very hard to know when your bearded dragon is having fun.

It is important to give it a good quality cage and to change the layout of its environment once every few weeks. Have a selection of different **hides** and rocks. After cleaning the **vivarium**, occasionally change the position of the rocks, making sure that you have a hide in the middle of the enclosure to prevent a feeling of insecurity. Empty cardboard boxes and cartons will be of great interest to your pet and serve a useful purpose in keeping it stimulated by its environment.

It is very tempting to take your pet out of the cage for long periods of time whenever you are at home. But you should only handle your pet once a day at the very most. It is better to handle it only once every two to three days. It won't forget you or suddenly become unfriendly.

The arrangement in the vivarium can be changed occasionally to provide stimulation for your pet.

You can decorate a cardboard carton and put it in the vivarium as a new hide for your lizard.

Does my bearded dragon like to be handled?

It can be very hard to know if your pet is happy for you to pick it up and cuddle it. Watch its behaviour. If it is bobbing its head or its beard turns a darker colour then put it back in its cage. Reward your lizard when it goes back to its vivarium with a favourite snack. But remember it is more likely that lizards put up with being handled rather than actually enjoying it.

You can keep a track of your lizard's behaviour and how often you handle it by marking it on a calendar.

31

Keeping my lizard healthy

Before buying your lizard talk with a few veterinarians in your neighbourhood to see whether or not they are happy to deal with your type of pet. All veterinarians are qualified to deal with **reptiles**, but some may prefer to refer you to a colleague with a special interest in these animals. This can be expensive and might involve travelling some distance depending on where you live. There are no special **vaccinations** necessary for either you or your lizard, but it is advisable to let your doctor know that you are keeping reptiles, and make sure that your **tetanus** vaccine is up to date.

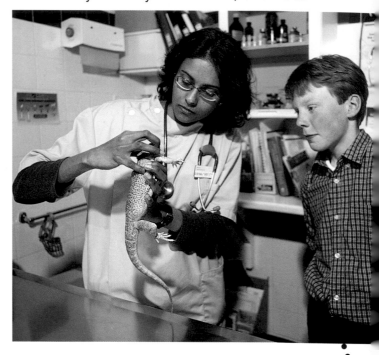

If you have a male bearded dragon there will be no need to have it **neutered**. If you have bought a female and don't intend to **breed** from her then this may need to be done later in life should she have problems laying her eggs. It may be difficult to tell the sex of your new pet if it is a **hatchling**. Don't worry, most single animals will be perfectly healthy without neutering. However it is worth making sure that you know what to do and who to contact in the event of an emergency.

If your lizard is sick you must take it to the veterinarian who will examine it and prescribe the relevant treatment.

Can I prevent common diseases?

Most health problems in lizards are caused by poor care and cage **maintenance**. Over 90 per cent of reptile diseases do not occur in the wild, only in captive animals. This shows you how important it is to give your reptile good food and change its **ultraviolet** tubes regularly. Make sure the temperature in the cage is correct and that there is an area where it can cool down. It is also important to have your bearded dragon wormed at the veterinary clinic twice a year to prevent possible illnesses.

This lizard looks alert and healthy. You must observe your pet every day for any signs of ill health – early diagnosis means early recovery.

Worming of lizards can be done orally.

33

Zoonoses

When you look after your lizard be careful about keeping yourself healthy too. **Zoonoses** are diseases that may be transferred from animals to humans. The best-known reptile zoonosis is infection by the bacteria *Salmonella*. The very young, very old and people who are unwell are most at risk of picking up an infection from reptiles. To avoid this, follow some simple rules:

- Wash your hands with an antibacterial handwash after handling any reptile, cage or accessory.
- Wear gloves when cleaning enclosures.
- Disinfect cages regularly.
- Keep young children away from reptiles. Older children should always be supervised.
- Keep reptiles and their equipment away from food preparation areas.
- Clean bites or scratches immediately with an antibacterial preparation. If the cut is deep, consult a doctor.

Always wear rubber gloves when you clean the vivarium. Make sure you don't miss out the edges and corners of the cage as bacteria can hide there.

If your lizard bites you, ask an adult to help you disinfect the wound using antibacterial cream.

A darkened beard means stress. When this happens it is best to leave your lizard alone in a quiet room in its cage.

Some health problems

Poor diet or environmental conditions cause most diseases commonly seen in captive **reptiles**. Many of the problems with pet lizards are simply not found in wild lizards. The more a lizard feels at home in a well-planned cage, the healthier your animal will be.

Ear abscesses

These are a common occurrence. The normally flat, or slightly dented, eardrum swells outwards to form a bump. The cause is a **bacterial** infection within the ear. The treatment for this condition involves an operation, so if you think your animal is infected, consult a veterinarian.

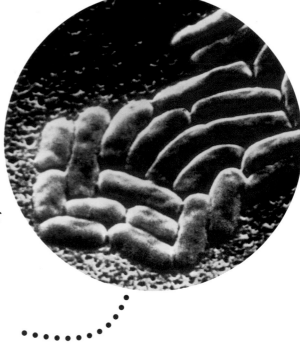

Infection of wounds by bacterial colonies like these can cause abscesses to form.

Other abscesses

Any wound that becomes infected can develop into an **abscess**. Common causes include poor hygiene, overcrowding and stress. If **territorial** animals, such as two males, are kept together with not enough space to form separate territories, one will attack the other and this may cause an abscess to occur. Treatment is by surgical removal of the abscess and making sure that whatever caused it is put right.

Metabolic bone disease

In this disease bones become low in calcium and break easily. Lizards who have it may suffer from fractured limbs, a swollen lower jaw, weakness in the limbs (a healthy lizard should be able to lift its body clear of the ground), loss of appetite, and in the later stages, collapse, muscle tremors and breathing problems. The causes are often linked to poor care of the animal, with lack of **ultraviolet** light and poor diet being the main reasons.

If badly affected, weekly calcium injections may be required. Some lizards can have a moderate to severe form of the disease, although their owners may be unaware that there is a problem.

Swollen legs like this one are often a sign that your lizard may have metabolic bone disease.

A lizard with a visibly diseased jaw. This is another symptom of metabolic bone disease.

Respiratory disease

Signs of respiratory disease include a runny nose, sneezing, wheezing, laboured breathing and open-mouthed breathing. A simple infection of the nose can easily become pneumonia if untreated. The most common cause is bacterial infection, although **viruses**, **fungi** and **parasites** can also be involved. Very sick animals require hospitalization for intensive treatment such as fluid therapy and force-feeding. Milder infections may respond to antibiotics alone.

37

Many antibiotics are made for **mammals** or warm-blooded animals, so if you don't increase the cage temperature the antibiotics may not work. Some viral and bacterial infections may be transmitted from you to your pet and so, if you are unwell, ask a member of your family or a friend to take care of your pet for a few days to reduce the risk of cross-infection. Keeping your pet clean will also help to reduce any risk of infection occurring.

A lizard receives a dose of antibiotics from the vet.

Internal parasites

A parasite is an animal that depends completely on another animal for its food and nourishment and to complete its life cycle. All **wild-caught** reptiles are likely to have internal parasites unless a sample of faeces has been taken and shown to be free from them. Parasites slow the animals' growth rates and make them more likely to contract diseases. It is sensible to worm mature animals at least once a year. If left untreated, parasites can cause death.

Nematode worms like these often infect lizards and can have very harmful effects on their health.

Worming is carried out by a veterinary surgeon either administering a solution placed inside the mouth, or by a small injection. This is often repeated after ten to fourteen days. Lizards with parasites may have different symptoms, such as diarrhoea or worms moving around in their faeces.

External parasites

Parasites that live on the outside of your lizard are called external parasites. Mites and ticks are commonly found and spread very quickly. These are blood-sucking parasites which, in large numbers, may cause **anaemia**. They may also contribute to the spread of other diseases between reptiles. These parasites enter the cage on your pet or on a piece of equipment that you have just purchased from a place where there is an active **infestation**. None of these parasites should be left untreated.

Ticks are relatively large so are easy to spot, although they may hide in big body cavities such as the nostrils. Individual ticks may be removed with tweezers, with care being taken not to leave the mouth-parts behind in the reptile's skin – this can lead to the formation of abscesses. It is better to get a veterinary surgeon to do this for you, though many experienced reptile-keepers will have carried out this procedure and may offer to help you.

This lizard has an infestation of ticks on its tail.

Mites are smaller and able to hide under single scales. They are often present in large numbers, and thrive on sick animals. Mites may be noticed crawling on the owner's skin immediately after handling the reptile, or floating dead in the water bowl.

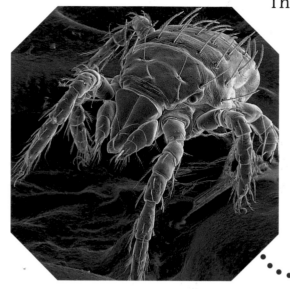

The mites do not generally bite people. A single female mite can lay between 90 and 100 eggs in spaces in the cage. This means that treating the cage as well as the animal is very important. There are many suggested treatments for mite infestations, but unfortunately none has proved 100 per cent effective and safe for both reptiles and keepers.

Mites are relatives of spiders and have eight legs.

Tail shedding

This is a way that many **species** of lizards escape **predators** in the wild. If a predator grasps the tail, it will drop off and often twitch to distract the predator's attention. This shedding of the tail does not harm the lizard, though it does cause some distress and should be avoided where possible. Eventually the tail will grow back, although it will not look identical to the original one! The old tail can be disposed of.

Tail shedding is a distress signal. Never hold your lizard by the tail as it may cause it to shed it!

Treatments to get rid of mites:

- Warm shallow baths. Bathing an animal for around 30 minutes will kill most of the mites on its body, although those around the head will escape. The water should be about 25°C.
- Dichlorvos ('Vapona'). This is sold in the form of fly-killing strips. These should be placed in the cage following the guidelines on the packet. Remember you will only need a very small piece of the strip inside a 120 centimetre cage! This method has the advantage of treating animal and cage simultaneously, but it can sometimes cause poisoning in both reptiles and their keepers. You must remove the water bowl during the treatment to avoid this.
- Ivermectin. This is only available from vets. It can be used in very small doses to treat individual reptiles by injection.
- Fipronil ('Frontline'). Available only through vets. This is a spray used as a flea and tick treatment for dogs and cats.

It is best to ask the advice of your veterinarian if you think that your lizard has mites.

A bath will get rid of most but not all the mites. You may need to use other treatments to get rid of the whole infestation.

Keeping records

To help decide whether your pet is growing healthily and developing well, it is important to keep accurate records on your computer or in a notebook. Over a period of time it is difficult to remember whether your lizard fed or went to the toilet on certain days in the past few weeks, let alone months.

Make a note of whether or not your pet has been eating. Remember that if it doesn't eat for a few days or more you may need to take it to the veterinarian to be checked over. There may be a reason why it has lost its appetite or that feeding has become difficult. It is very important to notice whether or not your pet lizard is going to the toilet; blockages of the bowel are very common and life-saving surgery depends on you noticing quickly that there is a problem.

Remember to get your family to take photos of you with your lizard.

You can make a colourful scrapbook about your pet using photos, drawings and notes about your time spent together.

Records can help to tell you if you may need to take your lizard to see the veterinarian, and copies of any notes should be taken with you if you decide to go to the veterinary clinic. This information will make sure that the veterinarian knows what is worrying you and can help to identify anything that is out of the ordinary.

Keeping a detailed record sheet will help you maintain up-to-date information about your pet's health.

Example of a record sheet:

Species . . . .

Sex . . . .   Age . . . .

Diet . . . .

Frequency . . . .

Temperature (day) . . . . (night) . . . .

Photo period – 12 hours

Key

Wt . . Weight in Kg

App . . Appetite

Th . . . Thirst

U . . . Urine

F . . . . Faeces

Date	Wt	App	Th	U	F	What we did today	Carer

Also, why not put photographs of the two of you together at different stages in your lizard's life to make a scrapbook? You can take this to school and show your friends all about your pet and how you care for it.

When a lizard dies

If you provide your bearded dragon with the best enclosure you are able to, and recreate its natural **habitat** to the best of your ability and give it a good diet, it should live for around seven years. It is possible for dragons to live longer and as equipment for keeping them in captivity improves, this is likely to be the case.

But no matter how well you care for your pet, one day it will inevitably die. Perhaps it will die peacefully in its sleep, or maybe there must be a joint decision taken by you and the veterinarian in order to prevent your lizard from suffering unnecessarily. It is never easy to decide when is the 'right' time to let the vet give an overdose of anaesthetic to send your lizard to sleep. Part of you will always want just one extra day to take your pet home and say goodbye privately. If your lizard is in pain, then as a true friend you will need to be strong and allow the veterinarian to end the suffering.

As your lizard gets older it may spend more time resting.

Feeling upset

Whether your pet passes away in its sleep or at the veterinary surgery, you will feel upset. It is perfectly natural to cry when you think of your pet leaving your life. You will have become very attached to your pet, and will miss it. But after a period of time the pain will become less and you will remember the happy times you spent together.

If your lizard becomes too weak due to illness or old age, you may have to make the difficult decision of putting it to sleep.

You can make a burial mound to mark your lizard's grave.

Glossary

abscess   soft lump filled with pus

anaemia   illness where blood concentration becomes affected

bacterial   caused by bacteria

bask   to lie exposed to warmth or sunlight

breed   to keep animals and encourage them to mate so they produce young

captive-bred   grown under the control of humans, not in the wild

contractions   shortening and thickening of a muscle

Cretaceous period   time in history when flowering plants first appeared and dinosaurs died out

dehydrate   to dry out or to lose water in the body enough to cause discomfort or illness

ectothermic   depending on external sources to keep body warm (cold-blooded)

fungi   types of living things that get food by absorbing other living or decaying material

genus   a grouping term used to classify animals or plants

habitat   place where an animal or plants lives or grows

hand-tame   brought up by humans with lots of time spent in training

hatchling   recently hatched infant

herpetology   the study of reptiles and amphibians

hide   place for animal to take shelter from predators, sunshine or rain

humidity   moisture in the air

incandescent   emitting light as a result of being heated

infestation   presence (of parasites) in large numbers, often causing damage or disease

komodo dragon   world's largest lizard

maintain   keep at the same level or rate, keeping in good condition by checking on something regularly

mammal   animal with fur or hair on its body that feeds its babies with milk

neuter   to perform an operation that stops lizards from having babies

parasite   small creatures, such as ticks and worms, that live on or in another animal's body and usually harm them

predator   hunter, animal that hunts and kills other animals for food

regurgitate   bring swallowed food up again to the mouth

reptiles   cold-blooded animals with scaly or rough skin

salmonella   a kind of bacteria

species   a kind or particular sort of living creature

substrate   soft material to put in the bottom of the lizard cage

territorial   defending an area of space that an animal sees at its own

tetanus   a disease caused by bacteria

ultraviolet light   invisible (to humans) part of light that is used to produce vitamin D3 in lizard's skin

vaccination   an injection that is given to protect against a disease

ventilation   allowing air to enter and circulate freely in a closed space

virus   type of micro-organism that causes illness

vivarium   cage for amphibians or reptiles

wild-caught   captured by humans from the wild

zoonosis   any disease that can be transmitted to humans from animals

Useful addresses

International Herpetological Society
c/o Mrs Carol Friend
15 Barnett Lane
Wordsley
West Midlands DY8 5PZ
United Kingdom
http://www.international-herp-society.co.uk

Exotic Animal Welfare Trust
Boundary Cottage Farm
Inkerman
Towlaw DL13 4QB
United Kingdom
http://www.eawt.org

More books to read

Lizard Care from A to Z, R. D. Bartlett (Barrons Education Series, 1997)

Reptiles and Amphibians, D. Alderton (Salamander Books, 1986)

Helpful websites

http://www.exoticpets.about.com/cs/lizardsaspets – Advice on how to care for lizards.

http://www.enature.com – Go to 'Reptiles' and then select 'Lizards'. Gives lots of information about different species.

http://www.anasid.org/mainlizards.html – Lots of information about different lizard species and how to care for them.

http://www.mavicanet.ru/directory/eng/18427.htm – Gives a listing of herpetological societies in the USA.

Index